FIELD TO FACTORY

Afro-American Migration 1915-1940

By SPENCER R. CREW

An Exhibition at the
National Museum of American History
Smithsonian Institution

February 1987 through March 1988

1987

To Marquette Folley-Regusters and Fitzroy Thomas,
tireless researchers, dedicated workers, colleagues, and,
most importantly, treasured friends.

*This publication is made possible by
a generous grant from Pepsi-Cola Company.*

The National Museum of American History also
gratefully acknowledges the support of the African
American Museums Association, the National Endowment
for the Humanities, and Delta Sigma Theta Sorority.

This publication is available from the
Department of Public Programs
National Museum of American History
Smithsonian Institution
Washington, D.C. 20560

Contents

Lillian Reuben-McNeary. *(Courtesy Carolyn Prioleau)*

Field to Factory

Lillian Reuben-McNeary moved to New York City without knowing exactly what to expect. Relatives there had promised to help her find a job and get settled. Any job had to be better than the frustration she had left behind in South Carolina. There she felt blocked at every turn. Lack of money and poor schooling opportunities doomed her hopes of training to become a nurse. Although it was difficult to leave behind her parents, brothers, and sisters, remaining in South Carolina meant abandoning her dreams.[1]

Lillian Reuben-McNeary was like hundreds of thousands of Afro-Americans who chose to move north between 1915 and 1940 in the hope of changing things for the better. Northern cities in particular attracted them because of the opportunities available there. Reports from northern black newspapers and from friends and relatives who had moved to these cities were encouraging. Northern employers paid blacks higher wages; northern school systems provided better educational facilities; and northern Afro-Americans could vote and even run for office. The advantages of life in the North and the hardships of life in the South were enough to set in motion the exodus now known as the Great Migration.

World War I and the Great Migration

The start of World War I opened up new economic opportunities for black workers. Before the war northern industrialists primarily relied upon the labor of native-born whites and European immigrants. Prejudice against black workers and limited demand for their labor made it difficult for Afro-Americans to find work. The fighting in Europe changed things. Demands on American firms to provide munitions and food for European customers increased as the fighting spread. At the same time, many European workers who might have

CONCRETE AMMUNITION

SECOND·LINE·DEFENSE

Gerrit A. Beneker

Direct appeals were made to Afro-Americans to take advantage of the new opportunities opening up to them in industry. *(Courtesy Smithsonian Institution)*

come to the United State chose instead to stay home and defend their homelands. Furthermore, in this country, the accelerating war effort siphoned off more of the industrial work force as men volunteered or were drafted into military service.

Faced with a shrinking work force, northern companies searched for another source of employees. They quickly began to seek out Afro-Americans living in the South, whom industrialists had occasionally used as strikebreakers in the past. Southern blacks represented a vast untapped source of labor. They were poorly treated by local white residents and they could fill unskilled jobs for these northern companies. As managers and company owners suppressed open prejudice against blacks to attract the workers they needed, news of the willingness of northern companies to hire black workers spread across the South.

Labor Recruiters

Labor recruiters provided one source of information about northern jobs. Hired by northern companies to locate southern black workers and bring them north, recruiters used a variety of tactics to entice

southerners. Most often they painted glowing, sometimes wildly exaggerated pictures of the benefits of moving north, emphasizing in particular the high wages paid by northern companies. Black recruiters also took advantage of their personal contacts in the black community. The Pennsylvania Railroad hired the Reverend James Duckery, a member of the black Philadelphia community, to travel to Florida to find workers. The Reverend D. W. Johnson, himself enticed north by a labor recruiter, returned to Mississippi at age seventeen as a recruiter for the Mobile and Ohio Railroad.[2]

The work was dangerous. Southern officials and employers feared the disappearance of their labor force and took actions to discourage recruiters. Laws were passed that banned recruiting under penalty of arrest or worse. The Reverend Mr. Johnson had several narrow escapes from southern officials out to stop local blacks from using the free railroad passes he had for them. He recalled:

But about twelve o'clock that door swung open and there was two great big, three great big red-faced guys. . . . Now they had a bullwhip on they shoulder and a rope and a gun in each of their hands. And those pistols, them barrels looked like shotguns, you know? They gonna kill every so-and-so Negro that they found had a pass. Well,

The shipyards on Hog Island near Philadelphia needed plenty of workers and paid good wages. *(Courtesy Smithsonian Institution)*

The Reverend D. W. Johnson, labor recruiter. *(Courtesy the Reverend D. W. Johnson)*

so they searched us one by one and they searched me. All but pulled off my shoe. Had they pulled off my shoe, that'd been it for me. Because they swo' they was gonna kill the ones who had it. Yeah, it was in the toe of my shoe.[3]

Although it is difficult to estimate how great an effect recruiters had on the northward movement of Afro-Americans, if nothing else, stories of their activities reminded southern blacks of the opportunities available in the North and the eagerness of northern companies to give them work.

The Black Press

Black newspapers were another source of information about opportunities in the North. The *Pittsburgh Courier* and the *Chicago Defender* actively encouraged blacks to leave the South. The editor of the *Defender*, Robert Abbott, migrated north in 1905 and founded the paper that same year. In headlines, editorials, advertisements, stories, and photographs, the *Defender* repeatedly pointed out the advantages of the North and played up the hardships of remaining in the South.

The widespread readership of the *Defender* testified to its popularity. By the early 1920s, Abbott claimed, he regularly distributed nearly 250,000 copies of the newspaper, up from an estimated circulation of 33,000 in 1916. The majority of his readers lived in the South and eagerly awaited the paper and its news of the North. In addition to using the mails, Abbott enlisted the aid of railroad porters and dining-car workers to circulate his paper throughout the country. Wherever they could, they left copies of the *Defender* for local residents. In this way southern readers continued to receive information about the North even when local officials banned the sale of the *Defender*.[4]

Letters and Visits Home

Even if northern black newspapers had been successfully suppressed in the South, Afro-Americans had other sources of information. Many southern blacks had relatives or friends who had moved north. These relatives frequently sent letters home filled with information about northern city life and describing what must have seemed to their readers to be a different world.

In the 1920s, for example, two relatives of Julia C. Hunt left

LATEST NEWS
If You See It In The Defender It's So

Chicago Defender
WORLD'S GREATEST WEEKLY

HOME EDITION

VOL. X., NO. 15.   SATURDAY   CHICAGO, APRIL 10, 1915   SATURDAY   PRICE 5 CENTS

DePRIEST IS ELECTED

Texas and moved north. Hunt's aunt moved with her husband to Chicago and Hunt's sister moved to Boston to attend music school. Both wrote Hunt regularly, and their correspondence offers a sense of the new experiences awaiting migrants. In Boston, her sister, R.V., met black people from Africa and the Caribbean, attended concerts with white friends, and earned a degree in music from a white school. Hunt's aunt in Chicago helped local Afro-American residents register to vote in local elections and traveled to Europe. Neither Hunt's aunt nor sister could have accomplished as much in Texas. As Hunt's sister wrote in one of her letters, "The only things I regret is that . . . I am so long getting here. I should have been here fifteen years ago, but better late than never I suppose."[5]

Similar correspondence came south from the men who joined the armed services and went north for military training. Their exposure to a different region of the country often changed their views of life in the South. And, if they traveled overseas, their experiences in Europe only reinforced their new perspectives on civil rights and racial equality. The lyrics "How you gonna keep 'em down on the farm after they've seen Paree?" had a special meaning for Afro-American troops from southern states. When they returned to the United States they found it even more difficult to accept the old restrictions placed on Afro-Americans.[6]

In addition to sending letters, former residents regularly returned home to visit family and friends. Homecoming celebrations sponsored by the church brought many people back. So did special occasions like weddings, christenings, and funerals. Children also traveled south for

The *Chicago Defender* brought news about the North to Afro-Americans living in the South. (*Courtesy DuSable Museum*)

extended visits with grandparents or relatives during the summer. Dressed in their nicest clothes, with plenty of money in their pockets, returning migrants sometimes painted irresistable, if unrealistic, images of life in the North and the prosperity awaiting anyone willing to leave. Even when their stories accurately described northern urban life and the limits to the improvements that most blacks could expect to find, the appeal of the North remained strong.

Labor recruiters, Afro-American newspapers, and relatives and neighbors who had moved north all helped persuade blacks to migrate. But perhaps equally persuasive were the conditions blacks faced in the South: segregation, discrimination, limited economic and educational opportunity, and violence.

Life in the South

After the end of Reconstruction in 1876, the nation's lawmakers and the Supreme Court turned their backs on southern-born Afro-Americans and left their rights as citizens in the hands of southern authorities. This abdication of national authority resulted in the creation of a two-tiered system of citizenship in the South: one set of rules for whites and a separate, more restrictive system for blacks. In this system of "Jim Crow" laws, Afro-Americans, under penalty of imprisonment and possible death, had to remain in special, separate sections on public transportation, in restaurants, and at movie theaters. The Supreme Court even gave its approval to this system of segregation when in 1896 in the case of *Plessy* v. *Ferguson* it upheld the constitutionality of "separate but equal" facilities for blacks and whites. In the South, as members of the Court well knew, separate was rarely equal.

Encouraged by earlier Supreme Court rulings, southern lawmakers also moved to restrict the citizenship rights of Afro-Americans. As they wrote new constitutions, many southern states added provisions that effectively, if sometimes indirectly, removed blacks from the voting rolls. Mississippi in 1890 adopted a state constitution that included a poll tax of two dollars and barred from voting anyone who could not read any section of the state constitution, understand it when it was read to them, or give a reasonable interpretation of it to the satisfaction of local election officials. These restrictions prevented a small number of whites—and almost the entire black population—from voting in Mississippi elections.

Colored drinking fountain,
Halifax, North Carolina.
(Courtesy Library of Congress)

Louisiana carried disenfranchisement of Afro-Americans one step further in 1898. In addition to high property and educational requirements to qualify to vote, the state introduced the "grandfather clause." Simply put, the grandfather clause exempted a person from the voting requirements of the new state constitution if his grandfather had voted in 1867. No Afro-American could qualify for this exemption since blacks were not allowed to vote in Louisiana in 1867. Strictly speaking, the "grandfather clause" did not exclude anyone from voting. But it enabled the state of Louisiana to write voting restrictions broad enough to disqualify most black voters and then exempted thousands of white voters from these same restrictions to ensure a vast majority of white voters at the polls.[7]

The Ku Klux Klan and other groups further reinforced the second-class status of Afro-Americans. Crosses burned in black neighborhoods, public lynchings, and other threats of violence were a constant undercurrent in the lives of southern blacks. Local officials often overlooked and sometimes condoned this violence. Their attitude left black families vulnerable and without recourse. Under these circum-

COLORED
WAITING ROOM

PRIVATE PROPERTY
NO PARKING
Driving through or Turning Around

BINGO
TONITE!

Good
Housekeeping

True Story
HITLER'S
LOVE LIFE
REVEALED
BY HIS
FORMER MAID

CAROLINA COACH COMPANY 45

Bus station, Durham, North Carolina. *(Courtesy Library of Congress)*

stances, blacks who appeared to defer to the system had a much easier time than blacks who defied it. Open rebellion resulted in swift punishment, a reminder to the rest of the black community of the consequences of breaking the rules.

Adhering to the rules forced Afro-Americans to remain constantly on guard for fear they might offend whites. Not stepping to one side of the sidewalk, refusing to overlook daily swindling by local store owners, simply being too successful economically, or any number of lesser offenses might result in an outbreak of violence. Afro-Americans in the South lived a precarious existence at the whim of local white residents. One misstep, as James Plunkett, a former resident of Virginia, pointed out, might result in disaster, "because they knowed that the least little thing you would do, they would kill ya. So they had to lead a quiet life. Had to walk a quiet life."[8]

Farm Work

Equally precarious was the economic stability of blacks living in the South. At the start of World War I more than two-thirds of the Afro-American population of the United States lived in the rural South. The majority of these people did not own the land they worked. They were either wage laborers, renters, or sharecroppers dependent upon their landlords for their livelihood. Sharecroppers, who made up the largest part of this group, received a portion of the crops they produced as wages to pay off any debts they may have incurred during the year. According to the agreements they made with their landlords, if they could not pay off their debts they faced confiscation of their personal property and possible imprisonment.

A farmer's chances of paying off his debts depended on the size of the crop and the price it brought. Most sharecroppers grew cotton

Hanging Tree, New Madrid, Missouri. (*Courtesy Library of Congress*)

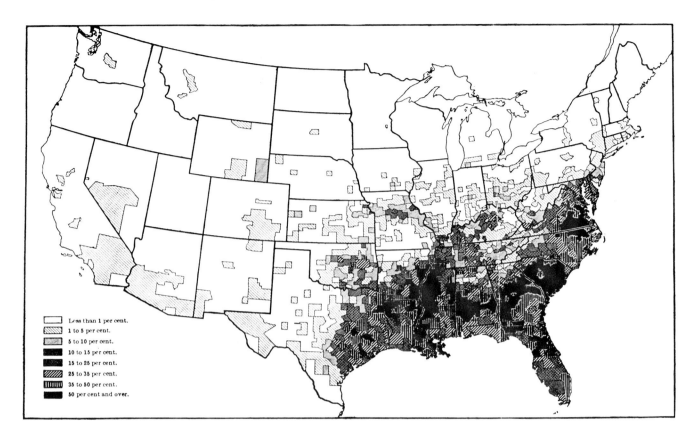

Legend:
- Less than 1 per cent.
- 1 to 5 per cent.
- 5 to 10 per cent.
- 10 to 15 per cent.
- 15 to 25 per cent.
- 25 to 35 per cent.
- 35 to 50 per cent.
- 50 per cent and over.

Percentage of Afro-Americans in total population of the United States by counties, 1910. *(Courtesy Library of Congress)*

Farming took long hours and hard work. A good mule was a necessity. *(Courtesy Library of Congress)*

as their cash crop; consequently, cotton dominated southern agriculture well into the 1930s. On small farms the entire family helped grow the crop. Carrie Millender remembered her own days working the family farm in Alabama very clearly.

Back there then most of the family was large with two and three boys in a family, and they had to work so hard. . . . I'm talking about hard work. They didn't have tractors. You plowed the mule. You hoed grass. . . . Picked cotton. . . . See that was hard.[9]

Cotton farmers plowed and planted in the late winter and early spring. Most farmers broke the land with a mule-drawn plow and used a cotton planter to sow the seeds. Simply designed, both the plow and the cotton planter were sturdy and easily maintained since an extended breakdown of equipment hampered planting and cut profits.

After the cotton plants sprouted, workers hoed the rows throughout the spring to thin out the plants and remove weeds. Field work slowed during the summer until September, when the plants ripened. Workers picked the cotton by hand, a task that demanded the labor of the entire

Harvesting the cotton crop demanded the help of the entire family. *(Courtesy Library of Congress)*

family. After picking the cotton they took it to a nearby cotton gin where the seeds were separated from the lint. Gin owners often accepted a portion of the seeds to pay for ginning costs and bought the rest to sell to seed crushers who marketed the oil and byproducts.[10]

In an economic system largely based on credit, the first cash many southern farmers received for their labor came from the sale of the cottonseeds. Many sharecroppers, however, received no cash from their seeds. Instead their landlords credited the value of the seeds against their accounts. Any cash sharecroppers received came after the cotton lint was baled, taken to market, weighed, and sold. Even at the time of sale, sharecroppers remained at the mercy of the landlords, many of whom owned or controlled the scales used to weigh the cotton. Unscrupulous landlords used weighted scales to undervalue the crop, deprive farmers of their just profits, and increase their chances of remaining in debt. Even when croppers knew they were being cheated they had few options. Moses Burse of Georgia explained the trap that ensnared many sharecroppers:

We went barefooted. My feet been frostbitten a lot of times. My dad couldn't afford to buy no shoes. He'd get in debt and he'd figure every year he going to get out. . . . They'd tell you, "you bought so and so," they get through figuring it up you lacking $100 of coming clear. What the hell could you do? You living on his place, you couldn't walk off.[11]

The cycle Burse described tied sharecroppers to the land and left them under the control of their landlords. Local laws favored the landlord in any dispute, leaving the sharecropper with little recourse but to accept his fate or suffer the consequences of open defiance. Even if they moved from one landlord to another, as many sharecroppers did, their debts usually followed them. Many landlords allowed sharecroppers to leave only if the new landlords paid their debts.

Escaping debt became even harder during and after World War I as natural catastrophes made it more difficult to grow an abundant crop. The most serious and widespread of these disasters was the boll weevil. This insect spread northward from Mexico and by the start of the war had devastated cotton crops in Louisiana, Mississippi, Alabama, Georgia, and Florida. The boll weevil destroyed young cotton bolls before they reached maturity, and so wiped out any chance sharecroppers had of making a profit. Nate Shaw of Alabama recounted the

Buying supplies at a plantation store. *(Courtesy Library of Congress)*

impact of the boll weevil on his 1923 crop: "Them old boll weevils stayed in my cotton until they ruint it. I didn't make but six good heavy bales and it weren't bringin' twenty cents."[12]

Disastrous floods in Mississippi and Alabama in 1915 added to the problems of some farmers. The flood waters destroyed crops, homes, and personal belongings and forced hundreds of sharecroppers and farmers off the land. Many of the dislocated farmers and agricultural workers left farm work completely.

Southern Schools

Poor educational facilities for their children also encouraged Afro-Americans to leave the South. Following the concept of separate but equal, the vast majority of southern communities created separate school systems for black children. Woefully unequal, these schools offered only minimal educational training. According to Hughsey Childs, who lived in North Carolina as a child, "When I was a boy, the state didn't even give you but three months to go to school. That's all. Three months, well, you could barely learn the alphabet in three months."[13] Along with an abbreviated school term, black schools did not receive their fair share of state educational funds. As a result, schools for Afro-American students were poorly maintained, meagerly equipped, and overcrowded.

Handicapped by these problems, Afro-American teachers sought to provide the best possible education for their pupils. Many students, like Elizabeth March, had fond memories of how hard their teachers worked on their behalf. "We only had one teacher from the first to the sixth grade and she taught all of us [80 to 90 students]. We was all in one little room, but they was some good teachers."[14] Unfortunately, many of these teachers, also products of the southern educational system, were insufficiently prepared for their duties and the conditions under which they were forced to teach. Their task was made even harder because landlords at times pressured sharecroppers to remove their children from school and put them to work on the farm. With school terms already shortened to accommodate the crop cycle, additional missed days only put black students further behind. By the time the average student dropped out of school in the fifth or sixth grade, he or she had received only a rudimentary education.

Playground games. *(Courtesy of Southern Historical Collection, University of North Carolina at Chapel Hill)*

Parents at times took their children's education into their own hands, sharing what knowledge they had. *(Courtesy Library of Congress)*

Lack of funds and poor equipment hampered the quality of education provided at black schools. *(Courtesy Library of Congress)*

For students who wished to continue their educations beyond elementary school, the options were limited. Since few public black high schools existed in rural areas or small towns, Afro-American students in their teens often had to attend private schools. Established by parents, philanthropists, and educators dedicated to providing educational opportunity for black students, schools like Piney Woods in Mississippi, Avery Institute in South Carolina, and Palmer Institute in North Carolina existed throughout the South. Of the few, lucky students who could attend these institutions, many had to board at the schools or travel long distances every day, sacrifices they endured willingly. The majority of Afro-American students remained trapped in inferior public schools or were denied an education altogether. The hope of improving their children's futures through a better education caused many parents to move north.

Piney Woods Country Life School, Piney Woods, Mississippi. *(Courtesy Piney Woods Country Life School)*

The Decision to Move

Despite the hardships of life in the South and the allure of a new beginning up north, the decision to move was seldom an easy one. Afro-Americans wrestled with the same problems faced by any people about to leave behind their homes, families, and familiar surroundings for a chance at a better life: Does one family member move first and find a place for the rest? Will we make new friends? Will we like living in a big city? Will we ever see our old friends again?

Embracing the unknown is rarely easy. And, despite the difficulties of surviving in the South, many people found a deep sense of security in their families, friends, and communities. Supportive Afro-American communities existed throughout the South in spite of the restrictions placed upon them by white society. These communities provided a buffer against a harsh and rigid system of racial separation and made it possible for blacks to live restricted but satisfying lives. Deciding to migrate, therefore, was never a simple matter of choosing whether to endure or escape segregation, a lack of economic opportunities, a poor educational system, and other problems. Personal and economic factors complicated the decision. The hardships of life in the South drove many people to leave despite the strong pull of family and community bonds. But for those who remained, and many Afro-Americans stayed in the South, these same bonds were strong enough to keep them home.

Family

Children learned important skills while working with their parents. *(Courtesy Southern Historical Collection)*

Family and home life complicated the decision to leave. The economic well-being of the rural farm family depended on the labor of the entire household. Children helped with crop production, child care, household chores, and outside jobs. Women generally oversaw the care of domestic animals, the family garden, young children, and the household. They also helped in the fields or took in washing to add to the family income. Plowing, planting, hoeing, and harvesting required most of the time of adult males; general maintenance of tools, fences, and farm buildings filled the rest.

The interdependence that developed between parents and children working closely together made the family a powerful socializing agent.

Tenant child and her play-house. *(Courtesy Southern Historical Collection)*

As they worked with their elders, children learned important skills they would need as adults: how to plow a straight row; how to cook poke salad; how to survive in the midst of racism. Clashes did develop between parent and child as the younger generation at times rebelled against their elders. But these disagreements, too, were part of the learning process.

The tight quarters on many farms also helped to produce close-knit families. Few Afro-Americans owned the houses they lived in; most houses were supplied by the landowners for whom they worked. The majority of these dwellings were small, one- or two-room wooden-frame house or cabins constructed in the "dogtrot" or "shotgun" styles typical of rural housing throughout the South. Most family activities took place in the largest room, which served as a kitchen, playroom, washroom, workroom, and bedroom. Other activities spilled onto the front porch or in the yard, where family members often gathered to discuss the latest news, tell stories, or enjoy the evening breeze. Sarah Jones had very fond memories of the time she spent with her grandmother.

But my grannie was a lively old soul. She used to tell us all kinds of things about what her life in slavery. She was a wonderful dancer. She would entertain her mistress and her guests so many times. And it was quite common that she could dance very well. My grandmother could dance with a cup of water on her head and never spill a drop. She tap danced and taught us how. It was a great pleasure to see my grandmother dance and hear her talk about slavery times. I tell you it was wonderful.[15]

The many hours spent together created an intimacy that made the family an important source of support, consolation, and advice for its members.

Community and Church

People also turned to their neighbors if they needed help. The small size of rural communities reinforced neighbors' reliance upon one another. In Lillie Whittaker's neighborhood in Florida, when "You got sick and there was somebody there to clean your house, somebody there to wash your clothes, somebody there to fix your food if you had children, somebody to fix your food if you didn't have no children."[16] In the isolated areas where rural blacks lived, this kind of support was invaluable. Everyone endured hard times at one time or another, and the support of neighbors eased the struggle.

In rural communities the church was the center of most social activities. The church house itself sometimes served as a school, a meeting place for fraternal organizations and other groups, or a site for picnics and fairs. Most importantly, however, it was the site of regular church services.

Many church members traveled miles each week to gather in worship. The service also gave the members of a community the chance to exchange information. Because of the demands of agricultural work, friends might not see one another for weeks at a time. Church offered a break in the routine and a few hours away from the farm in the company of family and friends. According to Carrie Millender of Alabama, "we were glad to get to come to church because that's when you saw your friends."[17]

The ministers of these churches were among the most respected and best informed members of many rural communities. Their visits to church members in the community and their travels to regional and national conventions gave them a broader perspective on local and national events. Many were inspirational speakers, and their congre-

He is Risen

Church services took families away from the isolation of their daily routines and brought them together with their neighbors and friends. *(Courtesy National Archives)*

gations enjoyed hearing them preach. Before she left Virginia for Philadelphia, Minnie Whitney looked forward to Sunday sermons.

Those preachers that preached there were old time preachers, some of them couldn't read or write good; but, they was called by God. All they would tell you was where to find the text and close the Bible up and preach a sermon out of this world.[18]

Church members also eagerly awaited the news they received as part of the church service. Through their travels, ministers learned about former community members who had moved away and about the opportunities available in northern cities. Some ministers used this information to discourage migration, focusing on the hardships of northern urban life. Other preachers encouraged members to move and provided letters of introduction to sister churches in the North.

Church buildings also provided meeting places for schools, fraternal organizations, and other groups. *(Courtesy Library of Congress)*

Annual church events like homecoming attracted visitors from nearby areas as well as from northern locations. *(Courtesy Library of Congress)*

Homecoming celebrations also provided news about the North. Sponsored by the church and usually taking place in mid or late August, homecomings brought together present and former church members. The activities usually filled an entire day beginning with prayer meetings in the morning followed by midday and evening services. Between services congregants picnicked and talked. Many family members and friends who had left returned to renew old ties and show their successes. Invariably they appeared in their best clothes and full of stories about the advantages of life up north. In many ways homecoming epitomized the conflicts at the heart of the decision to leave. The sense of fellowship generated at this event reinforced people's roots in the community at the same moment that visiting migrants gave glowing reports about the North and the opportunities there.

A vibrant and supportive Afro-American community existed in the South despite the hardships and burdens borne by black residents. This separate community protected children and taught them survival skills in a hostile environment. It provided for neighbors during difficult times. It created places of refuge for friends to gather with loved ones and escape the struggles of everyday life. It offered reasons for sticking things out in a bleak situation. It is what kept many people in the South despite the ample reasons to move. For hundreds of thousands of Afro-Americans, however, moving North represented a chance at a new life. So they severed the friendships and family bonds of a lifetime, and left.

Heading North

A migrant's place of residence in the South often influenced where he or she settled in the North. Since most migrants had little money, they used the cheapest and most direct route north. Afro-Americans living along the Atlantic seaboard usually traveled up the East Coast to live in cities like Philadelphia, New York, and sometimes Boston. Many residents of Georgia and Alabama settled in Cleveland, Pittsburgh, and Detroit. Mississippi and Louisiana residents frequently relocated to Chicago.

Railroads like the Illinois Central, the Pennsylvania, and the New York Central carried many migrants north. Train travel was relatively

inexpensive if migrants took advantage of the special promotions railroad companies offered. Because many companies gave special fares to groups of people riding together, migrants often formed "clubs" that capitalized on these group rates. Migrants also took advantage of special excursion fares between certain cities. The Illinois Central, for example, sold cut-rate tickets between New Orleans and Chicago.

Afro-Americans who worked for railroad companies enjoyed a special advantage since railroads regularly issued passes for free travel to their employees. Workers interested in relocating in the North used these passes to transport themselves and their families. Rufus Crew, an employee of the Southern Railway, used this method to transport his family to Cleveland.

Traveling by train also had disadvantages; black railroad passengers traveled in segregated cars in the South. Since these cars were located near the locomotive, passengers who opened their windows for fresh air received a shower of soot and cinders. In addition, people in these

Packed and ready to head north. *(Courtesy Library of Congress)*

"special" sections received little or no service. On overnight trips they were barred from sleeping cars and had to rest as best they could in their seats. Unable to buy food on the train, they purchased quick meals during stops or brought their own food in a basket or cardboard box.

Thousands of migrants also traveled north on buses, automobiles, and trucks. Along the East Coast, many migrants sailed on ships between southern ports and cities like New York and Washington, D.C. Traveling by water was slightly less expensive than train travel and included sleeping quarters in the price of the ticket. Many young men hired on as deckhands and worked their way north.

A Journey in Stages

No matter which form of transportation migrants used, they rarely left on the spur of the moment. Some decided to leave quickly during the early war years when free train tickets were easily available or when faced with threats of violence. The Reverend D.J. Johnson moved north because:

I was drivin' this team for this old man. He paid me $5.00 a week and previous to that I had worked for another one for $2.00 a week. And I left and worked for this one for $5.00 a week, and this old man's boys, they threatened me. If I didn't come back and work for the $2.00, I was in danger, see? So they even set the time that they were gonna come and get me. And they were gonna get me on Monday and I left Sunday night.[19]

For most migrants, however, moving north required time, planning, and money. In many families, one member went north first, found a job and a place to live, and then sent for the remaining family members. This method kept members of a family separated for long periods of time and entailed a risk that they might not see each other again, in part because local authorities in the South sought to prevent blacks from leaving by intercepting letters and sending travelers home from the train station. One South Carolinian recalled that she, her sisters, and her mother had to send their clothing ahead and pretend they were taking the train to visit a friend in a nearby town. It was not until they arrived at a train stop outside their own town that they could safely buy their tickets north.[20]

For migrants who could move north without interference, the cost of the trip still meant months and even years of saving money. Traditionally, the slow season, when the maturing plants needed little care, allowed many southern blacks to take on additional work. Farm workers found jobs at logging camps, sawmills, factories, construction companies, and in private homes in both the North and South. Usually the money they earned helped pay the bills and keep the family going until the crop was harvested. But when the family planned to move north, this money helped pay for the trip.

Southern cities like Birmingham, Savannah, and Memphis attracted many of these seasonal workers. Employers in these cities looked forward to the workers' arrival since the slow season coincided with the busiest time of year for many businesses. Most workers took these positions for several weeks and then returned home for the

During the growing season black farmers often found additional work in local companies like this tobacco plant to supplement the family income. *(Courtesy National Archives)*

Coal mining offered another means of obtaining extra income. *(Courtesy Library of Congress)*

In the South, most Afro-American women employed outside the home worked as domestic servants. *(Courtesy Penn School Collection, Penn Community Services, Inc.)*

harvest. But others found that they enjoyed working for cash rather than credit and never returned to the farm.

Migrants worked their way north in stages, moving first to a small town or larger southern city to earn enough money to move their families. Reaching their final destinations could take months or even years. But moving in stages had at least one advantage: working in southern cities exposed Afro-Americans to an urban industrial environment and prepared them for life in northern cities.

Even when they took the time to plan carefully and save for the trip north, migrants rarely reached their final destinations with much money in their pockets or more clothing and personal belongings than they could carry in a few pieces of baggage. Transportation costs, while not exorbitant, depleted much of the money migrants saved. And, unless they already had a place to stay with room for their furniture, there was no reason to bring furniture and other large items north. Many migrants arrived in the North in the same condition as Lilly McKnight, who brought

just some clothes, that's all. Suitcases, that's all. I sold and gave away all of my furniture, but I didn't bring nothin' but my clothes, that's all. Just packed a suitcase and got a train and came on up here. That's nerve isn't it?. . . . I had a little [money], about 100 dollars. It didn't take much money. I've forgot how much train fare was. But I had enough to carry me over till I got a job.[21]

Up North

Escaping the South did not guarantee a happy ending for migrants once they arrived in the North. A sometimes overwhelming array of new sounds, sights, and decisions immediately confronted them. When Burrell Caldwell, a migrant from Mississippi, made his first visit to downtown Chicago, the city dazzled him:

Then I went downtown that following Saturday to see some of Chicago—this was down on State Street and Lake. There I saw the Chicago Theatre. After leaving the country I had just left—and seeing a million lights in front of the theatre, and hearing the beautiful organ played by Jesse Crawford inside—it was just beautiful. That was in the year of 1923, and after seeing that, I wrote my mother and said, "If Heaven is as beautiful as that theatre and that music, I'm ready to go there now!"[22]

Mr. Caldwell quickly found a job and eventually brought his parents to the city. As did many migrants who moved north first, he

New arrivals to Newark, New Jersey, 1918. *(Courtesy Newark Public Library)*

also helped find employment and housing for other family members who followed him.

Not all migrants were as fortunate as Burrell Caldwell. Con artists took advantage of many new arrivals, either swindling them or attempting to draw them into a life of crime. Young women in particular were the targets of unscrupulous schemes. In response to these problems, women's organizations in many urban areas set up special programs to protect newly arrived single women as well as unaccompanied women and their children. The Philadelphia Association for the Protection of Colored Women provided shelter and help

National Urban League
meeting, 1923. *(Courtesy
Smithsonian Institution)*

for women new to that city. In many cities, the National Urban
League, church groups, Traveler's Aid Societies, and other local
charitable organizations provided temporary housing, job information,
day-care facilities, and guidance to migrants who arrived unescorted
and bewildered.

The National Urban League, founded in 1911, in particular sought
to respond to the economic and social needs of migrants. Branch offices
throughout the country launched programs that located housing,
boycotted firms that refused to hire Afro-Americans, trained newcomers
for industrial jobs, and conducted surveys seeking to solve problems
of health and crime in black neighborhoods.

Reports issued by the Urban League and other organizations
reveal that migrants brought tremendous changes to northern cities.
Before the Great Migration, northern Afro-Americans had lived in
multiracial neighborhoods located in various parts of their cities.
Because of their relatively small numbers, they had only limited impact
upon the larger community. The arrival of thousands of blacks in these
cities led to spectacular increases in the size of urban Afro-American

populations and the emergence of large, predominantly black enclaves such as Harlem in New York and the South Side in Chicago. Between 1910 and 1920, the black population in New York City increased by 66 percent, in Chicago by 150 percent, and in Cleveland by 400 percent. A combination of racism and the inability of large numbers of blacks to afford the higher rents in other parts of the city locked most blacks behind ghetto walls.[23]

Housing

Housing in the black sections of the city often was dilapidated and lacked adequate sanitation. Many ghetto residents suffered health problems and a higher-than-average death rate from diseases like tuberculosis. Overcrowding added to these problems as many tenants, due to their low wages and the housing shortage, shared their homes with boarders.

Boarders, many of whom were relatives or friends temporarily staying with a family while they found their own lodging, served a practical purpose. If boarders were working adults, they provided extra income. If they were unemployed or a young adult they babysat, kept house, or cooked so that other family members could work. Although space, health, and personal problems sometimes caused by boarders disrupted households, boarders made a crucial difference in the economic stability of many families.

Migrants, despite their housing difficulties, did not let their physical surroundings overwhelm them. Just as they had in the South, migrants added special touches—photographs, family Bibles, home-made quilts—to their northern homes to make their houses more personal and remind them of their previous way of life.

They also applied old customs to new circumstances. In rural areas the porch or the front yard had an important function. The lack

of space in tenant homes in the South pushed family and social activities outdoors. Washing, cooking, eating, and other activities all occurred regularly beyond the walls of southern rural homes. Migrants modified these activities for northern urban life.

Especially during warm weather, overcrowding and poor ventilation drove many city dwellers out of their homes and onto their porches and steps. The "stoop" then became an extension of the home. It let neighbors communicate easily with one another. Passersby might chat with friends or learn the latest news as residents prepared food, read letters from back home, or enjoyed the outside air.

A Mixed Reception

For many newly arrived migrants, the adjustment to northern life was difficult. As Delores Sheppard described it, one needed time to feel part of this new community.

I didn't like it when I first came here. It was hard for me to get really adjusted to the people and what not. And then, as time went past and I saw myself getting adjusted and I made more money than I had down south. And that's really why I got myself adjusted.[24]

Nor did all northern residents welcome the newcomers. Whites, who faced added competition for jobs and housing, at times responded violently to their new neighbors and initiated several racial conflicts. Three of the most highly publicized took place in East St. Louis, Illinois, in 1917, in Chicago in 1919, and in Detroit in 1925. The Chicago riot began in June 1919 when a black teenager was struck by a brick while swimming outside of the "colored" section of Lake Michigan. Thirty-eight people died during the four days of rioting, 537 people were injured, and nearly 1,000 were left homeless. The Chicago riot was just one of several outbreaks of violence against blacks during the summer of 1919.

White residents also turned to legal devices like restrictive covenants to control the sale of homes in their neighborhoods. In these pacts property owners agreed not to sell or rent their homes to Afro-Americans or anyone else their neighbors found objectionable. Segregation persisted in other areas, too. The signs weren't there, but the customs remained. In fact, the extent of discrimination often surprised migrants like Rebecca Taylor:

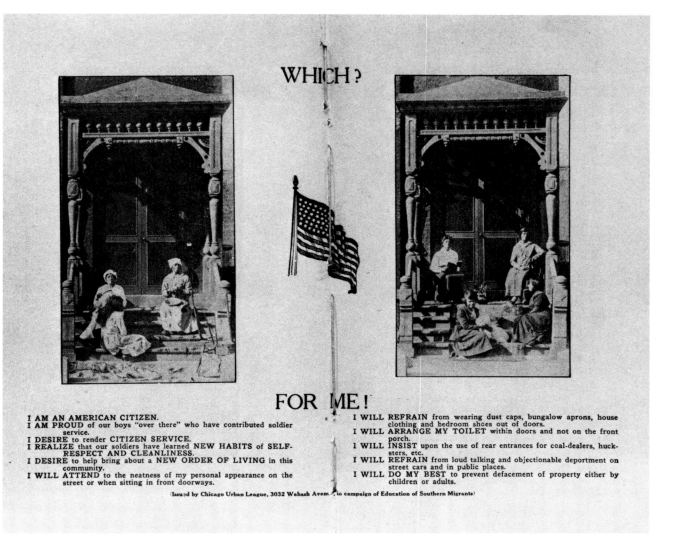

WHICH?

FOR ME!

I AM AN AMERICAN CITIZEN.
I AM PROUD of our boys "over there" who have contributed soldier service.
I DESIRE to render CITIZEN SERVICE.
I REALIZE that our soldiers have learned NEW HABITS of SELF-RESPECT AND CLEANLINESS.
I DESIRE to help bring about a NEW ORDER OF LIVING in this community.
I WILL ATTEND to the neatness of my personal appearance on the street or when sitting in front doorways.

I WILL REFRAIN from wearing dust caps, bungalow aprons, house clothing and bedroom shoes out of doors.
I WILL ARRANGE MY TOILET within doors and not on the front porch.
I WILL INSIST upon the use of rear entrances for coal-dealers, hucksters, etc.
I WILL REFRAIN from loud talking and objectionable deportment on street cars and in public places.
I WILL DO MY BEST to prevent defacement of property either by children or adults.

(Issued by Chicago Urban League, 3032 Wabash Avenue, in campaign of Education of Southern Migrants)

When I came to Plainfield I discovered that Plainfield was as segregated as the South. It was almost the same but the only thing I guess was you didn't have to sit in the back of the bus. You could sit any place on the bus. But, everything else was just like it was down south. I didn't see any difference, because the theaters were segregated, the hospitals were segregated, the churches of course.[25]

Flyer distributed to Chicago migrants by the Chicago Urban League. *(Courtesy Library of Congress)*

White residents were not alone in their concern about the impact of Afro-American migrants. Northern blacks, too, had reservations about the newcomers. They worried that the growing number of new arrivals would increase discrimination and physical restrictions. The unsophisticated manners of the migrants were a special concern. Established residents urged the newcomers to forget their rural ways and adopt more "acceptable" behavior. Organizations in several cities mounted campaigns to encourage this transition.

The Chicago branch of the National Urban League, for example, launched several campaigns to teach migrants the duties of citizenship. Hundreds of women traveled to the homes of newcomers to talk with them about the importance of hard work, proper decorum, and good housekeeping. A flyer distributed by the league in 1919 made these points even more graphically. In bold print the flyer proclaimed "Which For Me" and offered a series of choices between adopting the more sophisticated dress and actions of proper city dwellers or maintaining rural fashions and customs. The point of the message was very clear. If newcomers hoped to gain acceptance in their new places of residence they had to adopt the proper code of behavior.[26]

Factory Work

Along with instructions on proper behavior in public places, the Urban League also offered practical information about finding and keeping a job. Many migrants found their new work world unsettling. Time clocks, assembly lines, and piecework were new experiences for workers accustomed to the openness of the outdoors and the seasonal rhythms of farming. Agricultural work, although rigorous, allowed flexibility in meeting deadlines connected with producing a crop. It was important to get the field prepared or the seeds planted or the crop harvested by certain times, but sharecroppers measured their productivity at the end of the season by the size of the crop, not daily. To receive full paychecks each week, factory workers had to produce every day.

Northern industry, guided by efficiency experts, emphasized punctuality and steady productivity. Time had a different value in the industrial world. Every second was precious. Only so much time was allotted for lunch, for breaks on the job, or for time away from the job. Workers normally put in ten-to-twelve-hour days, six days a week. A worker's pay often depended on how much he produced in a day or whether he kept pace with the assembly line. Any absences for vacations or sickness meant smaller paychecks. The machines that controlled how fast people worked, how much they were paid, and when they rested symbolized the importance of time in the lives of industrial workers. Even migrants who had some experience working

Spray-painting lacquer on Ford car bodies. *(Courtesy Henry Ford Museum and Greenfield Village)*

in sawmills, steel companies, or fertilizer plants in the South were not totally prepared for the rigid routines imposed on them by northern companies. Management styles and production routines in steel companies, for example, varied from company to company and from region to region. Although a southern steel worker might understand the techniques of making steel, he still had to adjust to the production patterns of a new company.

For agricultural workers entering industrial work for the first time the adjustments were more radical still. Time clocks forced them to arrive on the job at precisely the same time each day. If they arrived late, their paycheck reflected the lost hours. If it happened too often, someone else took their place. In many of its admonitions to newcomers,

Garment workers got paid for each piece of work they completed not for the number of hours they worked. *(Courtesy National Archives)*

the Young Negroes' Progressive Association of Detroit emphasized the importance of punctuality, good work habits, and regular attendance on the job. A card they passed out to new workers emphasized in verse the importance of adhering to the time clock and adjusting to a new work situation.

> *He watched the clock*
> *He was always behind*
> *He asked too many questions*
> *He wasn't ready for the next step*
> *He did not put his heart in his work*
> *He learned nothing from his blunders*
> *He was contented to be a second-rater*
> *He didn't learn that the best part of his salary was not in his pay envelope*[27]

Worker in a meat-packing plant in Cincinnati, Ohio. *(Courtesy Ohio Historical Society)*

Workers in many industries had to adjust to production quotas or assembly-line speeds set by management as well as to the time clock. In the garment trades, workers were paid for each piece of a garment they produced. The faster they worked, the more money they made. This method encouraged workers to finish more items, but it also increased the pressure on them, especially when companies reduced the price per piece. Other industries used similar techniques to increase productivity and lower costs. One stockyard worker in the sheep-killing department complained about a supervisor who took one man off the job but refused to slow the assembly line, making the remaining men work that much harder.[28]

Some migrants fresh from the country reacted to what they considered unreasonable treatment by working for a few days or weeks

at a time or repeatedly switching jobs in the hope of finding better working conditions. Lilly McKnight took a job in a Philadelphia factory, but did not stick with it.

This factory was one where they was makin' blouses and shirts for men and women. You got paid for so many garments. I was pressin', I wasn't makin' them. It just didn't suit me. You knows what suits ya and wasn't suit ya. You want to be satisfied in what you do. If you aren't then you want to do somein' else, right?[29]

Especially during World War I, many industries needed workers and switching jobs was relatively easy. Even after the war ended and the demand for labor decreased, job opportunities still existed. In most cities, one or two companies dominated the local economy and provided most of the industrial jobs for Afro-Americans. In Pittsburgh steel manufacturers dominated the economy; in Chicago the packinghouses and in Detroit the automobile industry employed large numbers of people. In the latter city the River Rouge plant owned by the Ford Motor Company hired more Afro-American workers prior to 1935 than any other automobile manufacturer. It also was the only plant to employ Afro-Americans in assembly-line work, although the majority held janitorial or unskilled foundry positions.

The work Afro-Americans found in the North often was dirty and dangerous. This Ford worker is grinding rough spots off freshly molded metal parts. *(Courtesy Ohio Historical Society)*

To maintain a steady flow of workers, Ford and other auto companies developed a strong working relationship with Afro-American churches in Detroit. The ministers of these institutions in effect became recruiters for the auto industry, and their recommendations almost assured employment. This system gave church members a means of finding work for relatives moving north and enabled Ford and other manufacturers to maintain a steady stream of workers. Companies in Pittsburgh, Philadelphia, and other cities worked out similar arrangements with Urban League officials or local black leaders to help assure a steady supply of black workers.

Industrial positions available to Afro-American laborers generally paid more than agricultural work. But black employees in northern plants rarely rose to skilled occupations or supervisory positions. The jobs available to them often were backbreaking, monotonous, low-paying, and offered little chance for advancement. Nearly nine of every ten Afro-Americans employed in industry worked as common laborers. They also held jobs that demanded more rigid patterns of work. Meat processors in Chicago, steelworkers in Pittsburgh, automobile workers in Detroit, and garment workers in New York City all had to remain constantly alert to the machinery, tools, and people around them. Molten steel, sledgehammers, skinning knives, and sewing machines rarely forgave human error. One misstep could result in a lost finger, a broken limb, or even death.

Blue Jenkins worked at a grinding machine in a factory in Racine, Wisconsin. At times the grinding wheel came flying off the machine and spun wildly across the factory floor. Fearful for his safety, Blue remained ever vigilant against these occurrences. But, while he avoided losing an arm or a leg to the machine, it took a toll on him in other ways:

You'd have goggles on, naturally, because of sparks flying, but when you'd take off your goggles you'd just see the part where your goggles were and all the rest of your face would be black and your lungs. You'd just spit up big clots of dirt.[30]

Discrimination on the Job

To avoid promoting black workers, many employers used the excuse that blacks did not have the skills or motivation to handle demanding work. Studies of Afro-American workers found, however, that given the opportunity Afro-Americans could handle more difficult work and were eager for the chance. The industrial secretary of the Chicago Urban League found that blacks performed well when advanced to higher positions. As with white workers, incentive played an important role in the careers of Afro-Americans. Workers who felt they had some chance to earn extra money and advance within the plant performed more efficiently. Workers who felt they had no chance for advancement had little pride in their work and often did not remain on the job very long.[31]

Many white workers feared the competition for jobs created by the addition of blacks into the labor pool. Especially after World War I, as soldiers returned from Europe, the competition for jobs increased. Although many blacks lost jobs to returning soldiers, others had proved their value as workers and kept their positions. Blacks were an accepted part of the work force by the 1920s and posed more of an ongoing threat to white workers than they had prior to 1915. The violence directed towards Afro-Americans during the summer of 1919 illustrated growing white concern as did the rebirth of the Ku Klux Klan in the 1920s in many northern communities.

Blacks and Unions

Much more effective than riots and Klan rallies in slowing the entrance of blacks into higher-skilled and better-paying jobs were labor unions. Many unions had clauses in their constitutions that excluded blacks from membership or relegated them to separate unions with little influence. The stated policy of the American Federation of Labor forbade the inclusion of unions that had discriminatory provisions in their constitutions, but in reality several member unions, such as the Brotherhood of Railway Carmen of America and the International Association of Machinists, excluded blacks. In many companies, unions exercised considerable influence over which workers filled skilled

When Afro-Americans joined unions they helped strengthen the bargaining power of the organizations. *(Courtesy AFL-CIO, George Meany Memorial Archives)*

positions. The anti-black attitudes of unions made it nearly impossible for Afro-Americans to attain better-paying jobs.

One of the reasons for the antipathy of some labor unions towards black workers was the use of Afro-Americans as strikebreakers. During the steel strike of 1919 in Pittsburgh, blacks workers for the most part refused to leave their jobs and support white strikers. Management in fact shuttled blacks from plant to plant, which aided in the defeat of the strike.[32] Strikers saw these actions as deliberate attempts to break their unions and perceived black stikebreakers as collaborators with management.

In many strikes, blacks brought in from other parts of the country did not realize they had been hired as stikebreakers and sometimes quit when they learned the circumstances of their work. But most of them saw it as a chance to get jobs in areas previously denied them and took advantage of the opportunity. Afro-Americans frequently felt the same as a foreman in a Chicago factory, who stated: "Unions ain't no good for a colored man, I've seen too much of what they don't do for him. . . . I tell you they don't mean nothing for me."[33] Many labor union members, on the other hand, felt they should exclude blacks because of what they saw as an anti-union bias. Union officials in Pittsburgh believed, "in the entire steel industry, the Negroes, beyond compare, gave the movement less cooperation than any other element, skilled or unskilled, foreign or native."[34] These conflicting attitudes made it difficult for many unions and Afro-Americans to work together.

The United Mine Workers, the International Ladies' Garment Workers, and several other unions recruited Afro-Americans into their ranks. By organizing all the workers in their industries, they gained the clout to extract improvements for their entire memberships. Although often insensitive to issues of race, these unions did provide benefits for blacks who joined their ranks.

Not all migrants who moved north took jobs in industry. Afro-Americans also filled service positions, unskilled laborer jobs, some skilled positions, and a few professional openings. The majority of these positions, however, offered low wages, small room for advancement, and little job security. A drop off in business or a decision to reduce the labor force could leave Afro-American workers jobless. The struggle was not only to find work, but to find regular work.

Steady work was not guaranteed in the North, but neither had it been in the South. Northern salaries were at least two or three times

higher than those for comparable jobs in the South. Even with the higher cost of living in northern urban areas, migrants generally improved their real earnings. Despite their lack of security, northern jobs offered important opportunities to migrants. For Lilly McKnight regular work meant bringing her children to Philadelphia to live with her.

I didn't stay sittin' down. I went over to the unemployment office and got myself a job. I knew I had a responsibility. It's up to you to face your own responsibility. Don't try to put it on anybody else. My children was in the South and I was up here, so you know I had to scruffle around to do the best I could to bring my children up here. And I did.[35]

NEW JOBS FOR WOMEN

Everyone is getting used to
overalled women in machine shops

Women have made good as
Street Car Conductors and Elevator Operators

Clerical Work
quite a new job for Negro Girls

Slav, Italian and Negro Women
making bed springs

The war brought us
Women Traffic Cops and Mail Carriers

Laundry and domestic work didn't
pay so they entered the garment trade

Black Women at Work

Lilly McKnight found work as a domestic, as did most Afro-American women who worked outside the home. Even with the new jobs available to women because of the labor shortage caused by World War I, race and sex limited the industrial opportunities available to black women. As with black men, northern companies offered black women work only on the lower rungs of the occupational ladder, and when the war ended the number and variety of the few opportunities dwindled. So many women took positions as domestics, nannies, cooks, and laundresses. Although these jobs paid as well as or sometimes better than comparable occupations, they required long hours, carried low status, and demanded deference to an employer.

Some women, like Lois Crew, took these positions in order to earn money for other things. When Lois moved to Cleveland, Ohio, as a teenager she took a job as a domestic. She spent five years in this job while she attended night school. With the money she saved from her salary, she entered Normal School at Ohio University and received her teaching certificate. After graduation she obtained a teaching position in the Cleveland public school system. Lois Crew's career path indicated the importance of finding a job and hanging onto it. Her story also points to one of the few professional areas open to Afro-American women—teaching. Domestic work for Lois served a function that her sister Madie, who later became a nurse, summed up very clearly: "I did domestic work, too. I hated it, but it was a means to an end."[36]

Not everyone who entered domestic service hated the work, but they almost universally disliked the hours of a live-in servant. Household workers who resided in the homes of their employers were constantly under scrutiny and on call. Day work, which enabled women to return home each evening, increased the independence of servants. It allowed domestics to see their families every night rather than only on the weekends. It also placed clearly defined limits on the hours of the workday, which for live-in servants commonly stretched on long into the evening.

Day workers rarely wore uniforms; instead, they brought their own work clothes, usually a housedress. At the end of the day they changed out of their work clothes and returned home in their traveling attire, carrying the housedress in a bag. For many women, not wearing

Lois Crew benefited from her move north. *(Courtesy Madie Crew)*

Black women also hoped to enter new occupations as a result of migrating. *(Courtesy National Archives)*

53

Just as in the South, the majority of Afro-American women in the North who worked outside the home had jobs as domestic servants. *(Courtesy National Archives)*

a uniform and returning home each evening represented an important increase in personal independence and an upward step in the ranks of domestic servants. One woman expressed the importance of the change in status very clearly, "When I got to carry clothes I was finally working in what I wanted to. . . . I was proud to put my stuff in a bag at home. I guess I wanted to finally show I didn't wear a uniform, I wasn't a servant."[37] Because of the advantages of day work, more and more women insisted on it when they accepted domestic employment.

Black Churches in the North

Northern black churches benefited directly from the increased freedom afforded day workers. The extra time available to day workers allowed them to participate more extensively in the activities of their churches and added an extra vitality to these institutions.[38] Because religion created a vital link between their old and new lives, the church served a particularly important function among migrants. In the South, the church was an essential part of the community life of rural residents. Finding the right church after they moved north, therefore, was imperative. Migrants needed to feel comfortable at church services and with the members of the congregation. The more their new church reminded them of home, the more it seemed a refuge from a strange and sometimes hostile urban environment.

Shiloh Baptist Church, Newport, Rhode Island. *(Courtesy Rhode Island Black Heritage Society)*

Afro-American worshipers in Pittsburgh, Pennsylvania. *(Courtesy G. Dwoyid Olmstead Collection, Smithsonian Institution)*

Services in established northern black churches, however, differed substantially in style from services in rural churches of the South. Services in more reserved northern churches often lacked the emotional, exuberant vitality of rural southern worship. Minnie Whitney, who moved from Virginia to Philadelphia, noticed this about the church she first attended, "I went to the church and I seen the man, he took his text and he was reading the script. So I couldn't get used to that when I first came here. I was use to them closin' the bible and go ahead and preach."[39] Some northern black churches, put off by the migrants' outgoing religious style and generally lower economic status, discouraged migrants from joining their congregations.

The majority of northern black churches, however, did not discourage migrant members. Many welcomed the newcomers and set up programs to help them get settled. Tindley Chapel in Philadelphia, under the guidance of its minister the Reverend Charles A. Tindley, established programs to help migrants find housing, sometimes in the homes of church members, and receive academic instruction as well as training in a trade. Himself a transplanted southerner, Tindley had great sympathy for the plight of migrants and sought to ease their transition into northern urban life.[40] The Reverend Wade McKinney at Antioch Baptist Church in Cleveland, Ohio, and ministers of churches in Chicago, Pittsburgh, and other cities created similar programs to aid newcomers.

Migrants also founded churches of their own to continue their traditional forms of worship. Some were evangelical institutions that often attracted individuals from the same area of the South who shared similar experiences and religious points of view. Offering more than religious uplift, these institutions were places to share frustrations and centers of political and labor activities. The Pentecostal Church and the Church of God in Christ in Milwaukee, the Church of Christ, Apostolic Faith in Harlem, and similar institutions in various northern cities attracted strong followings among migrants.[41] These churches and others with large migrant congregations provided emotional and moral support for congregants and made it easier for them to cope with the constant pressures of city life.

Nannie Helen Burroughs

Nannie Helen Burroughs set out to help with the challenges facing black women when she created the National Training School for Women and Girls in Washington, D.C. Founded in 1909, the school stressed the importance of spiritual as well as practical training for black women. Along with academic and religious training, students acquired skills in bookkeeping, sewing, and domestic science. Burroughs believed black women had a special role to play in the destiny of Afro-Americans and trained her students to serve as models for the race. "We must have a glorified womanhood," she said, "that can look any man in the face—red, white, yellow, brown or black, and tell of the nobility of character within black womanhood."[42] To accomplish this end, Burroughs traveled across the country raising money on

Banner for the National Training School for Women and Girls. *(Courtesy Smithsonian Institution)*

behalf of her school and steadily enlarged it from a single building to a campus. The only trade and professional school for black women in the nation, the National Training School attracted young women from all over the country. Burroughs gained national prominence for her strong belief in self-help and her dedication to the advancement of black women. The school stood as a symbol to many Afro-Americans of the value of a good education both to the individual and to Afro-Americans in general.

Education in the North

In the eyes of many Afro-Americans education was the key to progress. An important reason many migrants left the South was the desire for better schooling for their children. Northern schools, because they had more money to spend, generally had better equipment and larger staffs than their southern counterparts. In addition, compulsory education laws in most northern states encouraged students to stay in school rather than drop out and go to work as black students often did in the South.

While northern schools had advantages over southern schools, they, too, had problems. Some northern school systems were segregated by law, and black schools received less funding than white institutions. Although many cities did not officially segregate their schools, residential patterns led almost inevitably toward segregation in education. New York and Chicago did not have segregated school policies, but school boards in Philadelphia; Dayton, Ohio; Gary, Indiana; and Camden, New Jersey, operated segregated schools. In all these cities,

however, predominantly black schools existed prior to the Great Migration. The presence of additional migrant children worsened the problem. Generally, the higher the percentage of black students in a school, the lower the percentage of funds it received.

Northern schools, despite their shortcomings, offered better training for black students than did southern schools. Migrants and their children took full advantage of these opportunities. Nearly twice as many black students completed northern high schools as finished southern ones, and many adults after moving north returned to school to complete their educations.

Schoolchildren in Chicago, Illinois. (*Courtesy Library of Congress*)

For both groups, children and adults, continuing their educations in a new system was not always easy. Shortened school terms and poor facilities in the South left many southern children behind northern students of the same age. Fellow students often teased children from the South because of their lower educational skills and their southern mannerisms. Scotty Piper had this problem when he moved from New Orleans to Chicago as a twelve year old. Constant teasing about his southern accent and mannerisms led to fights with his classmates. It took quite a while before he found a group of friends that accepted him and helped him adjust to his new surroundings.[43]

The New North and the New Negro

Migrants faced adjustments when they moved north, but they also altered the structures of the black communities into which they moved. Prior to the Great Migration, many successful black businessmen, politicians, and community leaders owed their prosperity and prominence to support from the white community. This interdependency tempered the public positions of these individuals because they sought to avoid alienating their white supporters. Blue Jenkins did not have a high regard for these early black leaders in his town, Racine, Wisconsin.

Well, the leadership in the black community wasn't the leadership in the black community as we know it today, where a black will get up and say certain things and have other blacks following him, backing him up. The black leadership wasn't that way then in Racine. The black leadership in Racine was this . . . when something was happening or [white people] wanted it to happen—the white people would come to this one individual and ask him what he thought about it or would he do something about it. . . . You had a white going to a black and a black speaking for the community, as such, who had no—no touch of the community—didn't know what really the community was thinking about. It was just his opinion—but this is the type of leadership that you had back then.[44]

Growing black populations in northern cities created new sources of support for community leaders. The new leadership, more dependent upon the black community than its predecessors, adopted aggressive stances on race and politics. Through political, economic, and legal pressure community leaders waged a continuous battle against racial discrimination. Alain Locke, a professor of philosophy at Howard University and a social critic, looking at the changes taking place as a

PUT THE
Spirit of Christ
In the Making
AND
Execution of Law

WE
HAVE
30,000 CLE

THE FIRST BLOOD
FOR
AMERICAN
INDEPENDENCE
Was Shed By A Negro
CRISPUS ATTUCKS

result of migration, commented, "the Negro of the Northern centers has reached a stage where tutelage, even of the most interested and well-intentioned sort, must give place to new relationships, where positive self-direction must be reckoned with ever increasing measures. The American mind must reckon with a fundamentally changed Negro."[45] Locke called this new generation of urban residents the "New Negro."

This new resistance to second-class citizenship affected several organizations established for the benefit of Afro-Americans. The National Association for the Advancement of Colored People (NAACP), founded in 1909, and the National Urban League, founded in 1911,

Silent parade in New York City, 1917. (Courtesy Schomburg Center for Research in Black Culture, New York Public Library)

61

Marcus Garvey. *(Courtesy Moorland-Spingarn Research Center, Howard University)*

originated before the start of the Great Migration. Both organizations developed programs that responded to the needs of migrants.

The Urban League sought to help migrants adjust to the difficulties of city living and to provide industrial opportunities for black workers. Under the direction of the national office in New York, branch offices across the country launched programs that located housing for migrants, boycotted firms refusing to hire Afro-Americans, and conducted sociological surveys of black neighborhoods.

While the Urban League emphasized economic issues, the NAACP focused more on legal concerns. NAACP members participated in boycotts and protest marches, such as the silent parade held in New York City against the 1917 East St. Louis riots, but they directed their major efforts towards dismantling the laws that supported discrimination and segregation. Throughout the migration period and afterward, NAACP lawyers initiated litigation that attacked voting restrictions, housing discrimination, and school segregation. The magazine of the NAACP, *Crisis*, under the editorship of W.E.B. Du Bois, relentlessly exposed and attacked the injustices against Afro-Americans in the United States.

The Universal Negro Improvement Association (UNIA), founded by Marcus Garvey, took a different approach to the problems facing blacks. Garvey, who came to the United States from Jamaica, attempted to give voice to the frustrations felt by many migrants trying to survive in a hostile environment. Believing it impossible for blacks to achieve equality in America, Garvey advocated a return to Africa. A dynamic public speaker with a keen understanding of the feelings of common people, he appealed to their self-esteem by emphasizing racial pride and solidarity and by creating economic and cultural programs run by his organization. After attending a UNIA meeting, one migrant wrote:

Yesterday afternoon I went to a meeting of the Universal Negro Improvement Association which is headed by Garvey. . . . They say without a country of their own, strong, able, and willing to protect Negroes everywhere, they will always suffer. I think they are about right about that. . . . I sometimes wonder if this organization is not the seed of a Nationalist movement of Negro Peoples? You should see their flag of pure silk in red, black, and green, the color runs across the flag, each a third of it. The black represents the Negro or black race, the red sacrifice, and the green eternal hope. Their songs are quite stirring and some parts are really wonderful.[46]

Under the auspices of the UNIA, Garvey launched several enterprises, including a shipping company, the Black Star Line; a newspaper, *Negro World*; and a factory for the production of black dolls. Many migrants supported him, and branches of the UNIA thrived in cities with large migrant populations, like New York, Philadelphia, Chicago, and Cleveland. Marcus Garvey's message had tremendous appeal for people disappointed by the realities of northern urban life.

Northern Politics

The presence of migrants in northern black communities also added to the political influence of Afro-Americans. The number of black elected officials at the local, state, and national levels steadily increased during the Great Migration. Forced clustering of Afro-Americans into segregated areas in northern cities created electoral districts that aided Afro-American politicians. A growing black electorate in Chicago helped send Oscar De Priest to the House of Representatives in 1928, making him the first black elected to that national body for more than twenty-five years. Other black officials gained local offices in New York, Pittsburgh, and New Jersey. Denied the chance to vote in the South, blacks took advantage of the franchise in northern elections.

Black voters also provided the margin of victory in several local elections. Their importance to politicians locked in tight contests resulted in outright courting of black voters and patronage appointments for many Afro-American politicians. Black voters understood the impact of their political influence and organized voter registration drives. In 1928 Mrs. L. A. Johnson wrote home to Texas explaining her participation in the election that spring. After helping in the registration for the primary election, she served as an official at the election itself.

Had to be at the polls at 5:45 a.m. Tuesday and sit there under the strain as a Judge and work too from the above hours until 8 a.m. The following morning without stopping to eat or drink, and then get up from such a posture and take the reports and Ballots to the City Hall and turn them over to the Board of the Election Commissioners, and such a crowd you have never witnessed.[47]

Oscar De Priest. *(Courtesy Moorland-Spingarn Research Center, Howard University)*

Julia Ward Howe State Republican Club, Providence, Rhode Island. *(Courtesy Rhode Island Black Heritage Society)*

Northern Black Businesses

The Great Migration served the interests of the northern black business community, too. Growing black neighborhoods increased the number of customers available to Afro-American entrepreneurs. Many of these businessmen were themselves migrants who brought with them a tradition of serving a predominantly black clientele.

Newspapers, funeral homes, beauty-culture businesses, savings and loans, drugstores, and insurance companies in particular flourished. These businesses varied in size from operations like the Gibson Dining Hall in Rochester, New York, to larger enterprises like the Victory Life Insurance Company of Chicago run by Anthony Overton. The success of these businesses often made their owners influential figures, leaders in their communities, and spokesmen for the concerns of their neighborhoods.

Dr. Marjorie Joyner is an excellent example of a business person expanding her influence beyond the business world. Dr. Joyner, who operated her own beauty salon, migrated north as a child with her family. She first settled in Dayton, Ohio, and later moved to Chicago, where she met Madame C. J. Walker. Walker, a pioneer in the black beauty-culture business, taught Dr. Joyner her new techniques for styling black hair. A close friendship developed between the two women, and Dr. Joyner eventually became a national representative for the Walker company. During fifty-seven years with the company, she trained thousands of students and met with prominent local and national political figures, including Eleanor Roosevelt.

Also committed to serving her community, Dr. Joyner heads numerous charitable activities. Since 1929 she has served as chairwoman of the Chicago Defender Charities, which gathers food and clothing for the needy. In addition, she helped found the Cosmopolitan Church in Chicago, which includes a day-care center and medical facilities for local residents.[48]

Migrants like Dr. Joyner filled the ranks of professionals in northern cities as they followed their clients north or left behind a lack of opportunity in the South. These newcomers became important agents in the development of northern black communities. In Chicago, sociologist E. Franklin Frazier believed, "This group has become large enough to comprise a new leadership as well as a distinct class in the

Lewis & Sons moving company, Cleveland, Ohio. *(Courtesy Western Reserve Historical Society)*

Local restaurant, Cleveland, Ohio. *(Courtesy Western Reserve Historical Society)*

community. . . . This new class of professional and business men is setting the standards of behavior for the rest of the community."[49]

Singers, musicians, and other artists also moved north hoping to find more opportunity and a broader audience. Places like the Howard Theater in Washington, D.C., the Peking Theater in Chicago, and the Lafayette in Harlem; publications like *Survey Graphic*, *Opportunity*, and *Crisis*; and organizations like the Harmon Foundation provided forums for Afro-American writers and performers. Although a few of the performers who came north, like Louis Armstrong, achieved national recognition, many did not. Instead they performed primarily before Afro-American audiences within their own communities. Out of the efforts of these artists a new culture emerged that interpreted art, literature, and music from an urban, Afro-American point of view. Their vision of black life and culture looked at the accomplishments of Afro-Americans with pride and sought to express a unique cultural tradition within American society. It was out of this new interpretation

Dr. Marjorie Joyner's beauty shop. *(Courtesy Dr. Marjorie Joyner)*

WELCOME I.B.P.O.E.W.
HEADQUARTERS
KING TUT LODGE No.389
MARY B. TALBERT. TEMPLE No.257.

of Afro-American life that the cultural renaissances in Chicago, Washington, D. C., Harlem, and other cities developed.

New communities filled with vitality and energy emerged from the mixture of newcomers to northern cities and established black northern residents. A blend of cultural traditions of migrants and long-standing northern black institutions, these new communities spawned storefront churches, black-owned businesses, and a growing black professional class. Cities within cities, they created worlds separate from the larger urban centers of which they were a part and gave birth to a "New Negro," self-confident and filled with racial pride.

King Tut Lodge, Cleveland, Ohio. *(Courtesy Western Reserve Historical Society)*

New Amsterdam Symphonic Orchestra. *(Courtesy Henry Preston Whitehead)*

Black and White

As Afro-Americans reappraised their place in American society, they also forced whites to reexamine their views on race and social equality. Growing black communities placed new pressures on public officials and local residents to respond to the demands of Afro-Americans. Questions concerning the legal and civil rights of blacks no longer remained primarily southern issues. For the first time northern white residents faced significant competition for jobs, housing, and political power from black city dwellers.

This pressure from Afro-Americans continued to increase as their population swelled. The Great Migration created a new momentum toward change. Court cases directed against restrictive legislation chipped away at one source of discrimination. "Don't Buy Where You Can't Work" campaigns brought economic pressure on businessmen to hire blacks in establishments with a large black clientele. These activities and others initiated by Afro-Americans gave them a growing belief in their own ability to improve their circumstances. They also encouraged blacks to confront and change circumstances they found unacceptable. From the Great Migration emerged a new, more aggressive Afro-American community that demanded rights for its members as American citizens.

A Mixed Blessing

While migrants invigorated the northern Afro-American community, moving north did not always remedy their individual difficulties. Migrating proved a mixed blessing for most Afro-Americans. The North offered new opportunities, but not without new challenges. For a minority of migrants, the North never quite measured up and they eventually returned south or regretted not having gone back. James Plunkett, originally from Virginia, said, "I came up North to see it, but sometimes I wish I had gone back to Danville. They treat you fine and dandy if you stay on your side of the fence."[50]

For many migrants the chance to start anew outweighed any problems, and they embraced their new lives wholeheartedly. Like Minnie Whitney, they could not go back to the old ways: "When you don't know no better you accept it, after I left home and went to New York and went back home I couldn't accept those things that's why I would never go back [south] to live. . . . You see I had got freed."[51]

Other migrants, though not as emphatic as Minnie Whitney about the benefits of moving, were at least satisfied enough to remain in the North and take advantage of the opportunities it offered. James Jones moved to Newark, New Jersey, from Sumter, South Carolina, in hopes of finding better working and living conditions. When he arrived, he didn't like Newark, but stayed because of the job he got with the Pennsylvania Railroad. As he expressed it, "I didn't like it but it was better than what I could find anyplace else. Fifty cents an hour, eight hours a day. Good pay along in that time."[52]

The Great Migration initiated changes that continue to influence modern-day American society. The most important of these were the creation of large, predominantly black enclaves in northern cities and a growing sense of confidence, economic opportunity, and political power in the Afro-American community. The more aggressive struggle against inequality that emerged during the years of the Great Migration did not disappear as the migration lost momentum during the 1930s. It reappeared as strong as ever with the renewed migration from the South during World War II. From 1940 to 1960, nearly three million Afro-Americans left the South. Many of them traveled to West Coast cities, though midwestern and eastern cities received their share of new residents. Afro-American communities in Los Angeles, Seattle, and Portland more than tripled in size as a result of this new wave of migrants.

Making a place for himself
in the North. *(Courtesy
Library of Congress)*

Marchers at the 20th anni-
versary of the 1963 March
on Washington for Free-
dom and Jobs. *(Courtesy
Roland L. Freeman)*

These migrants, like those who came before them, left the South
with great expectations, some of which remained unfulfilled. Problems
with substandard housing, unfair employment practices, and social
inequality persisted, creating an underlying sense of frustration and
anger. These frustrations fueled the civil rights activities and the urban
rebellions of the '50s, '60s, and '70s. Building on the tactics of their
predecessors, the new migrants joined with black northern residents
and used boycotts, marches, litigation, and the vote to force changes
in American society. While the modern civil rights movement had a
momentum of its own, the activism that characterizes the Afro-
American community and the configuration of present-day American
cities was directly influenced by the generation of Afro-Americans
who moved north during the Great Migration. Their presence fundamentally changed American society and forced Americans, both
black and white, to think differently about questions concerning race
and equality. After the Great Migration, American society was never
again the same.

NOTES

1. Telephone interview of Lillian Reuben-McNeary by Spencer Crew, June 30, 1986.

2. "Goin' North: Tales of the Great Migration," Education Special Supplement, *Philadelphia Daily News*, February 4, 1985, p. E-5; Interview of the Reverend D. W. Johnson by Clem Emhoff on May 19, 1976, in Beloit, Wisconsin, for the Beloit Bicentennial Oral History Project. Interview located at the Wisconsin Historical Society.

3. Johnson interview.

4. Roi Ottley, *The Lonely Warrior, The Life and Times of Robert S. Abbott*, (Chicago, 1955) chaps. 9-12.

5. Letter from R. V. Hunt to Julia Hunt, May 30, 1928, in the Hunt Collection, DuSable Museum, Chicago.

6. Arthur E. Barbeau and Florette Henri, *The Unknown Soldiers, Black American Troops in World War I*, (Philadelphia, 1974) chap. 10.

7. John Hope Franklin, *From Slavery to Freedom*, (New York, 1967) chap. 15; August Meier and Elliott Rudwick, *From Plantation to Ghetto*, (New York, 1968) chap. 5.

8. Interview of James Plunkett by Charles Hardy III in Philadelphia, August 4, 1983.

9. Interview of Carrie Millender by Peggy Hamrick in Wilsonville, Alabama, July 17, 1984, for the "Working Lives" Project at the Archives of American Minority Cultures at the University of Alabama, Brenda McCallum, Project Director.

10. Pete Daniel, *Breaking The Land: The Transformation of Cotton, Tobacco and Rice Cultures Since 1880*, (Urbana, 1985) 3-4; Fred A. Shannon, *The Farmer's Last Frontier: Agriculture, 1860-1897*, (New York, 1945) 80-100.

11. Interview of Moses Burse on August 12, 1980, for the New Jersey Multi-Ethnic Oral History Project of the New Jersey Historical Commission, Giles Wright, Project Director.

12. Nate Shaw, *All God's Dangers: The Life and Times of Nate Shaw*, (New York, 1974) 228.

13. Interview of Hughsey Childs by Charles Hardy III in Philadelphia, October 24, 1984.

14. Interview of Elizabeth March by Peggy Hamrick in Metro Gardens, Alabama, August 1, 1984, for the "Working Lives" Project at the Archives of American Minority Cultures at the University of Alabama, Brenda McCallum, Project Director.

15. Sarah Clarke Jones, "Lifestory," *Glimpses Into Our Lives: Memories of Harrisburg's Black Senior Citizens* (Harrisburg, 1978) 1.

16. Lillie Bruce Whittaker, "A Floridan Comes to Pennsylvania," *Glimpses Into Our Lives: Memories of Harrisburg's Black Senior Citizens*, (Harrisburg, 1978) 32.

17. Millender interview.

18. Interview of Minnie Whitney by Charles Hardy III in Philadelphia, March 6, 1984.

19. Johnson interview.

20. Interview of anonymous individual by Giles Wright on August 19, 1980, for the New Jersey Multi-Ethnic Oral History Project of the New Jersey Historical Commission, Giles Wright, Project Director.

21. Interview of Lilly McKnight by Charles Hardy III in Philadelphia, August 2, 1983.

22. Interview of Burrell Caldwell by Daisy Greene in Chicago, May 24, 1977, for the "Greenville, Mississippi and Vicinity Project" sponsored by the Mississippi Department of Archives and History and the Washington County Library system.

23. V. D. Johnston, "The Migration and the Census of 1920," *Opportunity*,

A Journal of Negro Life 1 (August 1923): 237.

24. Interview of Mollie Sheppard by Delores Sheppard in Newark, New Jersey, November 15, 1979, for the New Jersey Multi-Ethnic Oral History Project of the New Jersey Historical Commission, Giles Wright, Project Director.

25. Interview of Rebecca Taylor by Myrna Wasserman in Plainfield, New Jersey, March 10, 1980, for the New Jersey Multi-Ethnic Oral History Project of the New Jersey Historical Commission, Giles Wright, Project Director.

26. *First Annual Report of the Chicago Urban League* (1917), 11; *Bulletin of the National Urban League*, vol. 9, no. 1 (January 1920): 20-21.

27. Emmett J. Scott, *Negro Migration During the War*, (New York, 1920) 133.

28. The Chicago Commission on Race Relations, *The Negro in Chicago, A Study of Race Relations and a Race Riot*, (Chicago, 1922) 390.

29. McKnight interview.

30. Interview of Blue Jenkins by Mr. Roeder in Racine, Wisconsin, January 3, 1974.

31. Chicago Commission, *Negro in Chicago*, 378.

32. Ira DeAugustine Reid, "The Negro in the Major Industries and Building Trades of Pittsburgh," unpublished masters thesis, (University of Pittsburgh, 1925) 11-12.

33. Chicago Commission, *Negro in Chicago*, 424.

34. Reid, "Negro in Pittsburgh," 11.

35. McKnight interview.

36. Telephone interview of Madie Crew of Cleveland, Ohio, by Spencer Crew, June 18, 1986.

37. Elizabeth Clark-Lewis, "This Work Had A' End: The Transition from Live-In to Day Work," *Southern Women:*

The Intersection of Race, Class and Gender (Durham, North Carolina, 1986) 24.

38. Ibid. 33-36.

39. Whitney interview.

40. Charles A. Tindley, "The Church That Welcomed 10,000 Strangers," *World Outlook*, (October 1919) 5-6.

41. Florette Henri, *Black Migration, Movement North, 1900-1920, The Road from Myth to Man*, (Garden City, New York, 1976) 187; Joe William Trotter, Jr., *Black Milwaukee, The Making of an Industrial Proletariat, 1915-1945* (Urbana, Illinois, 1985) 130.

42. Nannie Helen Burroughs, "Unload the Leeches and Parasite Tom's and Take the Promised Land," in the papers of Nannie Helen Burroughs, Box 46, Manuscript Collection, Library of Congress.

43. Telephone interview of Scotty Piper of Chicago by Spencer Crew on August 12, 1986.

44. Jenkins interview.

45. Alain Locke, ed., *The New Negro: An Interpretation*, (New York, 1968) 8.

46. Letter from R. V. Hunt to Julia Hunt, June 25, 1928, Hunt Collection.

47. Letter from L. A. Johnson to Julia Hunt, April 10, 1928, Hunt Collection.

48. "The Dr. Marjorie Stewart Joyner Collection, Premiere Exhibition of selected photographs and artifacts, February 4-22, 1985" (Chicago, 1985).

49. E. Franklin Frazier, "Chicago: A Cross-Section of Negro Life," *Opportunity*, (March 1929) 73

50. Plunkett interview.

51. Whitney interview.

52. Interview of James Jones by Mordell Goodwin in Newark, New Jersey, 1980, for the New Jersey Multi-Ethnic Oral History Project of the New Jersey Historical Commission, Giles Wright, Project Director.

Bibliography

Allan Ballard. *One More Day's Journey: The Story of a Family and a People.* New York: McGraw-Hill, 1984.

James Borchert. *Alley Life in Washington, 1850-1970.* Urbana: University of Illinois Press, 1980.

The Chicago Commission on Race Relations. *The Negro in Chicago: A Study of Race Relations and a Race Riot.* Chicago: University of Chicago Press, 1922.

St. Clair Drake and Horace R. Cayton. *Black Metropolis: A Study of Negro Life in a Northern City.* New York: Harcourt, Brace, and World, 1962.

Peter Gottlieb. *Making Their Own Way: Southern Blacks' Migration to Pittsburgh, 1916-30.* Urbana: University of Illinois Press, 1987.

Alferdteen B. Harrison. *Piney Woods School: An Oral History.* Jackson: University of Mississippi Press, 1982.

Florette Henri. *Black Migration: Movement North, 1900-1920.* Garden City, New York: Anchor Press/Doubleday, 1975.

Clyde Vernon Kiser. *Sea Island to City: A Study of St. Helena Islanders in Harlem and Other Urban Centers.* New York: Atheneum, 1967.

Kenneth Kusmer. *A Ghetto Takes Shape: Black Cleveland, 1870-1930.* Urbana: University of Illinois Press, 1976.

George W. McDaniel. *Hearth & Home: Preserving a People's Culture.* Philadelphia: Temple University Press, 1982.

Gilbert Osofosky. *Harlem: The Making of a Ghetto, 1890-1930.* New York: Harper Torchbooks, 1963.

Emmett J. Scott. *Negro Migration During the War.* New York: Oxford University Press, 1920.

Nate Shaw. *All God's Dangers: The Life of Nate Shaw.* New York: Knopf, 1975.

Allan Spear. *Black Chicago: The Making of a Negro Ghetto, 1890-1920.* Chicago: University of Chicago Press, 1967.

Joe William Trotter, Jr. *Black Milwaukee: The Making of an Industrial Proletariat.* Urbana: University of Illinois Press, 1985.

Carter G. Woodson. *A Century of Negro Migration.* 1918; rept. New York: AMS Press, 1970.

Design: Gerard A. Valerio
Typesetting: Monotype Composition Co., Inc.
Printing: Virginia Lithograph